Máighréad Medbh was born in Newca   in 1959. She has lived in Dublin, whe   in the Dublin Writers Workshop antho   *and the Sewer* and *Edible Houses*. S...   ....o performed her poetry with rock musicians at various venues in Ireland, including The Underground night club in Dublin. She currently lives in Belfast. *The Making of a Pagan* is her first collection.

the making of a pagan

Máighréad Medbh

THE
BLACKSTAFF
PRESS

BELFAST

First published in 1990 by
The Blackstaff Press Limited
3 Galway Park, Dundonald, Belfast BT16 OAN, Northern Ireland
with the assistance of
The Arts Council of Northern Ireland

Printed by The Guernsey Press Company Limited

Typeset by Textflow Services Limited

British Library Cataloguing in Publication Data
Medbh, Máighréad 1959–
The making of a pagan.
I. Title
821.914
ISBN 0-85640-455-1

to Gerry
thanks for the rock-'n'-roll

CONTENTS

A NEW PLACE	1
WOMB	2
MOTHER	3
HER LAP	4
A PEACH DRESS	5
A SCRAPE OF COUNTRY	7
THE SWING	8
SARDINES	9
THE HALL	10
TASTE	11
SOLDIER	12
A FLOW OF BLOOD	13
MAN	14
TURNING SIXTEEN	16
THE BOREEN	17
FIRST LOVE	19
MOTHER SHADES	21
BEAT	22
FIRST NIGHT IN DUBLIN	24
ON CALLS	26
ON THE RIVER	28
COMING OUT	30
P.M.T.	32
CRAWLING	34
ENGAGEMENT	36
NIGHTS WITH ANNE	37

THE GREENHOUSE EFFECT   39

F-ING OFF   41

KEEPING THE ANIMAL DOWN   42

ORIGINAL SIN   44

BABY SKIN   46

FEEDING THE BABY   47

SONG FOR AONGHUS   49

GERRY   50

NOTHING FOR GIRLS   52

EASTER 1989   55

THE FUCKING PONTIFF   57

OUR STREETS   59

THIRTEEN YEARS DEAD   65

A NEW PLACE

Like a forgotten nut
it broke
one night.
Crack.
I never had the knack
of walking by a chasm.
In I went and down.
First there was a juicy feel,
white pulpish feel.
Nothing like the smell of white
in a strange nut.
My first bed was there,
just under the shell.
Squalch.
It was nice then,
the shell pressing on the
juicy white pulp pressing on me.
Better than a downy bed
down down in the country.
Squalchy in dreams
I bounced, spluttered,
swept on,
slushed in gullies,
floated furrowed.
Dark I went and grey
through a ploughed tunnel.
But then I opened all my eyes.
A new place.

WOMB

The return journey is
the only journey there is,
from light and teeming space
in search of the dark place,
back.
But there is colour here,
treasures hung from the high walls,
a cave that would be black
but they and the hint of a door
prism it.
I pick up the thread
that led me back.
It pulls taut.
Down it in royal welcome
the treasures pulley towards me,
a blue satin bed-jacket
a peach dress
a white cardboard box
shaking with spools
a yellow tin box, flower-embossed.
How it was.

MOTHER

'Clack' go her glasses
down on her nose.
'Raatum' go her false teeth.
'Suck suck suck' on the thread
to thread a needle
to turn a hem
to shorten a dress for me.

'Swallow' say eyes
in a goldfish bowl.
National Health doesn't care.
They brace me up
deface me
open me
white my hair.

HER LAP

Her lap is a country
where promises hang open.
Across the long chasm
her magic apron
makes a bridge smelling
of baked bread and tarts,
vouches safe.

I want to hammock you,
shrink myself back baby-size,
listen close to the sway
of your full green tree.

Her lap is the place of all home
where all things fruit and die.

Can I play upon your notes
like before,
bounce happy on your knee
to the beat of
your one-tight, two-loose flesh?
Look, I can sing the tune —
die diddle diddle die . . .

I have become monster
in my own shadow,
pressing on your land
like this.

A PEACH DRESS

blue and white day
and a peach dress
oh and a cuddly black
smooth black and brown and white dog
and a white cat
and his one blue eye
and his one green eye
and waking up to the
purr purr purr
of blackie
deep among the sheets

bok clack whirr
against the wall
i am billy jean king
i know them all
white dresses and all
dresses i cut them
from paper
and hang them on dolls
white with golden stars
midnight blue pale pink
and a lime green

i will marry in lime green
like a wild nymph
fresh from the fields
still damp
i will marry my only only
I will dance for you daddy
one two three and a

one two three and a
ballet bounce and a twirl
and a purr purr,
pirouette

A SCAPE OF COUNTRY

In all the gathered globe
never was a country like this.
This is green below red
below yellow below white
below blue.

Down the boreen,
hedges hoard clusters of lush.
Places for fairies to sleep,
fairies tiny as pin tips.

Tonight the moon will rise,
like a piece of furze
flying from a hill fire.
It will make the sky
highwayman blue.

THE SWING

This is the best world.
The swing creaks back and toward.
I pretend piranha underneath
raise heads
but I raise feet
and stretch them out.

The sun makes pictures
of gooseberry bushes.
Scents come dizzy up for air,
spread a veil on shone hair.
I should wear a parasol.

I pick blackcurrants
in my slip,
squeeze none too tight.
Sugar plantations must be like.
Or naked grapes
in honeyed, purple,
French extremes.

SARDINES

our house is divided
one part for him
one for all of us
we're like these sardines
i'm twisting their key
to let them out
to let me in
like he twists her key
and she moves like he says
and she stays in at night
like i'd like to twist
a knife in his gut
especially on fridays
with one tin for him
and one for all of us

THE HALL

There is a long hall
where I and my brother wrestle.
I in my vest and navy knickers,
he in white shorts.
I am a brave and keep-out-the-towel
warrior.
But this is love.

He teaches me the world.
When alone, I make streets.
Shops with skimped bikinis
thrown in windows.
Soft somethings for high-gloss girls.

A long altar
where I marry my toys.
Teddies with dolls
in christening robes.
'*Ave Maria*' to you –
Queen of the May-be-someday
but anyhow a joy.

When day disperses,
the hall has reflected light only.
Father's call flies down it.
There is a rosary
waiting to be strung out.
Then, at least, to bed.

TASTE

Legs are pins
stuck in cushions.
Softer, warm.
A ruler seated between them
has a hot smell after.

Three fingers, like monkeys,
are climbing to the top
where great leaves fold
into a mushroom cap.

What gills I have.
Twiddle. Jiggle.
That starts a fruity feel.
Sniff, and sweet as apple tart.

My stomach has a knot.
What for?
Flake out the white –
mmm, need lots of sugar.

Or will you try
my own ear's honey?
Straight out and tangy,
the taste of me.

SOLDIER

How does he dare
to look in my direction?
How does he dare to put me down?
I am soldier
just like he was.
Stand back.
Left right, left right.
How the foot is shoulder high.
He will not stare!

I can be secret agent too,
bag over shoulder
like in the comic,
gun at hand.
I bob down by low walls,
shadow ash trees.
I see you.
You don't.
I hear at doors.
Nothing good.

Blast into stone houses.
Look I have dynamite
sizzling red at the tip.
I will slap it in his face
and run
and not regret.
Or hand grenade his mounted thighs.
Or die for his poison.
Or
Fucking Bastard
Burn his eyes.

A FLOW OF BLOOD

The dog sniffs up my leg.
I know what he smells,
Blood under my dress.
Will he tell?
The fishy smell,
The must-be-washed,
Clean my nakedness,
Tidy my mess.

I was waiting for this,
My secret importance.
Will it soak my pants,
Drip onto the ground,
        onto the tiles in church?
Will everyone know?

First among my friends –
I am become woman,
I suffer like saints.
My clothes held close,
I walk with care.
Delicate.
Wise.
Blessed.
Virgin.

MAN

'What a piece of work . . .'

Shakespeare

The abiding colossus
has one foot in my bedroom,
one where I play and read,
a hand where I cook
a hand where I sit to eat.
He sticks his head
through the roof of my house
and sings, perennial.
He nods down when I move,
saying,
'Take me with you when you stay.'

I learn the female is a clam to be forced
and she must never learn how it's done.
The soft are the only worth considering,
those who feed, wash socks,
listen to rambling wisdoms over pints,
hear unspokens.
Men know how the world can be pushed around.

Men make time tick.
We wait for them,
wane before clanged armour
and bounding white.
We turn them princes.
They cannot do without –
especially us pale pink,
no make-up, leafy
country girls.

Women make and mend,
ourselves also,
draw in our brains for fear of spill.
We are buttons on their best soutanes,
are hung, fine cruxes,
from their necks.
We wreath about their middles.

They carry huge loads
to the furthest army of great houses.
They climb, ass-burdened,
to steep thrones.
When they tire, troubled,
we sit and kiss and watch.

We must seep out in weeping rivers
but they will love-stroke us,
spark up the female fire,
move close like stalkers,
finally open us with a silent push.
We lie and lie before they come,
their tokens, tributes,
running at our skirts.

TURNING SIXTEEN

Always cycling.
Always wearing odd clothes
sent from America or passed down.
Summer dresses make the best wear.
In winter I have one good coat
and one for hacking.

The town girls have the latest,
faded jeans, jazzy tops.
They smoke too, on the hill to school.
I am better than that.
I smoke in my private room.

I must have the biggest arse in school,
flopping like unmoulded jelly.
My face is a tomato
when I am asked to speak.
My hair is always tossed.

There must be a secret.
Are they never cold,
must wear caps and flatten their hair?
How are their legs so brown?

How can I be a film-star
with my scar
and my yellow teeth
and my phlegmy throat?

THE BOREEN

From the inside of town, when the library's closed,
it's a good cycle home at night.
I'm all in my head with a girly dream
of boys and kisses and cars
and fields where lovers run and fall
and wedding rings and beds.
The millionaire's window has no blind,
you can see the designer stove.
Now and then the couple stand
at the slanted, tinted glass.
Across the road the living-room
of Brady's bungalow is all on show,
the children racing, dancing, turning wheels.
I can't imagine life without
a closed front door, a curtained night
and secrets in the room.

The street lamps run up to the road
we call the dark boreen.
That's the road my house is on.
It always strangely seems
that I live nowhere outside me
and no-one sees me be.
I veer the bike and turn towards home.
The boreen is pitch tonight.
My lamp is just a spear of light
that pierces out a path.
The leaves remind me of the dress
a queen of England wore.
My wheels are dancing minuets
across a whispered floor.

But what?

My hands tighten on the handlebars
Swerve
Bright stones?
Eyes black and white
In the middle of the . . .
Man's standing body
Staring
Says hello
Can he stop me?
Keep pushing
Pedal Pedal
He's speaking
Says 'Wait. Come here a minute.'
I think he's that O'Brien from the well
Pedal Pedal
Girls not safe
Mammy told me
Just last Friday, Margie
He pulled her knickers down
I must escape
My chest will spill out
The pounding pounding
Throat is blocked.
I'm getting there
Away Away
The light of home
I'm there
The gate sings shut behind
I'm at the door

He's home
Compose.

FIRST LOVE

The plumb-stomached summer of it
leaves me abstract,
piking vacant halves on hay cocks,
staring vastly down the field
to stamp his face on every frond
and shoot.

Last night, the dance,
a whirl candy, pink-floss time,
girl-massed, boy-crushed.
'Can I have this one?'
Or a hand poking,
a rude beck.
'Why not?'

Then him.
His head turrets the host,
black on dull.
I'm here.
Feel the rush-winding of my
sum and substance out to you.
He sees. A broad, farming face grins.
The skyward eyes.

He bows his head when we dance,
hangs his lips on my neck.
My closed lids make a cell of each move,
the legs brushed,
the hand angling up from the waist.
He can feel,
He can feel through my blouse.

He is all about me,
huge as darkness.

and then
locked on the stairs
the first
the soft spoonful palping
down tongue
clipped to the lifelong suck
curl slouch about the teeth
setting the inside lip dancing
like a harem
cuddled to the last delicious
strangle just above the heart

my own
the only ever
marry marry marry
white and gold
white and gold
his slow walk
his huge hands
his tongue on my neck
                    in my mouth

The new blue dress next Sunday
and a soft comb back over the ears.
He kisses my ears.
I have scrubbed this cup forty times,
soaked in suds,
the way he bubbled me up,
blew me into full, light air,
opened the window and
Puff

MOTHER SHADES

down where
the shades are
i pray her
not fade
into
days now
she hardly hears
the needs
i speak
a step toward
is
a step in wake
of a weird wind
i pray her
not rescind
her helping smile
her sounding look
that now seem
lookaway

BEAT

white steps
white day
steel white mountain

jump stair to see
her jump stair to see
her jump stair to see

hanging at the tiptop
pale eyed speaker of
the end of the low bend
she has been taken

no she is not
away no she is not
away no she is not

come black hole in
ashen day
skirl scrape
suck away all that
colours flowers stands
and lift me high
to heaviside
to bolt and thunder
spark and geyser
sweat and swelter
wave and ray

galloping drumbeat
hip hop tumble

how many pulses
all in the body
leg thrum hand thrum
eye in a vibrate
vamp in the fleshpack
where do i fly

fly to home where
she is less a beating
face a vision
cannot kiss a face
that's brazen
she's abating

she is meat
she is deadbeat
she is deadbeat
she is beaten
dead she is beaten
dead she is beaten
she is beat
she is dead

FIRST NIGHT IN DUBLIN

There's a girl in the jacks boxed to the wall. She's in her scrimped-for jumper and jeans, all brand-city-new. But god, does she look like she's rupturing inside. Even her knees are crying. She can't stand up, she's so brittle. Partly the drink, I suppose, but mostly she was getting cross-brained out there. What were they talking about but bosses' habits, jokes she couldn't understand (What's so funny about 'coming'?), half-made comments with a cute nod or a rat-tat-tat laugh. What was that he said? What's dope? What did he mean, 'Balls to you'? How can he talk like that? Balls are a man's test . . . But that man looked nice, sounded really intellectual too. But he hadn't even seen her – or maybe he had. Yeah, he smiled. Maybe he thought she was pretty and demure, not like the rest of them. The things they said! But she knows, she knows . . . nothing, blast it. She has never even heard of The Smiths, let alone their songs. Why can't they talk about sincere things, themselves, what they really think? Politics even. She knows about politics. She's great on theories. That Englishman she met in the parish hall at home thought she was the most interesting girl around, even though he was 34 and she was only 17. So did Brian. That's what he liked about her, he said. But that's not enough, is it? Brian said she should let herself go more, dance without self-consciousness, shake her hips. 'Don't be so stiff,' he said, and then he barely kissed her. Awake all night, lying on the bed, and he only touched her breast once, saying, after one minute, 'If you want to call a halt . . . ' Call a halt, my god, he's the one boy, the only she would nearly make love to. Oh and it's all such a starless time. She was a

stranger to everyone at home and now she's stranger
still.

So she's crunched up, a bunched primrose, wet all over
with the evening and battered by lovers' feet. She knows
she must leave this box – some rude person just said,
'Hey, what are you doing in there, playing with yourself?'
– so she dries up, hauls her body, conjures her best
I-am-perfectly-in-control-and-who-are-you look, and
slowly moves out.

ON CALLS

At eighteen it is hard to be a law enforcer.
I must knock on doors, enter and question.

At eighteen I am in the balloon of idealism.
I study humans through the microscope of myself.

They call me a guardian of the fund.
Picture me in armour and spear.

I am rehearsed in de-focus.
Every time I knock on a door
I imagine myself elsewhere.

**FILE: Imelda Makum. Report of death received.
Pension book cashed for four months after
date of death.
By whom? Recover debt.**

A thin woman answers. 'No, I'm no relation. She lived
alone in her flat.' What next? I have an oblique mind. Oh
a niece? Where? Excellent. Thank you and goodbye. I
reach the house, a weighted feather.
'Oh the book? Yes I did. Wasn't I entitled to it? She was
a crochety old bitch. No matter what I did, she com-
plained. She was bedridden for the last year, wouldn't go
into hospital. Mother of Divine Jesus, I deserve to be
canonised after her. I washed her, fed her, cleaned up
her slops. Running from here to there, she ringing me in
the small hours over nothing. My life is ruined after her.'
This I cannot help. I stare at the file. You'll have to pay it
back, I'm afraid. No way out.

'But I got no allowance for looking after her.'
Sorry, you should have claimed one.
Out in the air the day is still fresh and blue and white. I am off on a daydream. Will he phone? Oh please let him phone.
The way he kissed my neck. I dream him the father of my children. Now Sharon, listen to your daddy.

FILE: Mary Anne Brady. Unmarried mother.
Review this case re change of address.

She is not expecting me. A man opens the door. Two other men are sitting in the only-apart-from-the-bedroom. The child runs dirty, half dressed, in circles. I have not studied the file. My god, she shares my birthday and she looks an old woman. Eighteen in a balloon. Any contact with the father? 'No, I don't know where he is. He ran off when he heard I was expecting.'
I am conscious of the three men in the not-the-bedroom. Brothers, I suppose. I hope. There are too many to be of significance. They could be friends. Some men and women are friends, they really are. I should ask. I am playing for time.
'They're my brothers in the other room.'
Great.
Claimant's brothers, I write, were present on the occasion of my visit. No sign of co-habitation.
I'm damned if I'm going to search her wardrobe and under the bed.

Sky again. Almost time for lunch and a read of the paper. I must read that article on the Japanese social system. I must write him a love letter.

ON THE RIVER

Summer on the Shannon
where it's always holidays.
Boat to boat,
bow to stern.
We are girls alone.

We moor the boat
and down to the pub,
where the hard-working men
from the power station
wear white shirts and denims,
large medals to show off wide chests.
They eye us, sweet-as-pie us.
The one I get is strong,
talks like a gentleman,
sings a song.
I sing.
We drink and the crowd sways
and the crowd becomes one
and oh the world is merry.

He kisses me on the German's boat.
I note the navy sky.
I throw up over the side.
He leads me home.

Back at our boat
the rain is flooding the fo'c'sle,
the boat is rocking,
Mary asleep in the other cabin,
I in my clothes on the top bunk,

he in my clothes on top of me.
Men always kiss and feel
and I don't really understand
what's next.
I am an operation body.
'What are you doing?'
My hand feels something fleshy and long.
That's the penis.
That's what I want to forget.
They don't really have one
that sticks right up and into you.
The water sweeps against the sides.
I am surrounded.
And he's still on top.
'I don't want to have sex or anything.'
I am drowned by the high tide.
What is that pain?
I think my scream will bring
the river running, send the birds calling,
but no, the water keeps sweeping,
the rain keeps battering
and I never screamed like this
and I never felt such pain

It's summer on the river
in the rain.
I can't tell,
I'll never know
if he came.

COMING OUT

my hands began it
and now I love it
my cunt is swelling
thinking of it
thinking of a tongue on it

a warm ache between my legs
my hands begin
stroke up my breasts
my breasts are steaming
nipples standing staring
my hands are drawing the world
from the mound of my head
to the round of my small toe
feel my legs
the inside thigh beginning
to blush then shining
then my stomach a mass of tingle
I touch my clit it sings
a touch is a step inside
I am queen and land
where east meets west
my hands unclose a passage north to south
my face is full upon me
all of me my face
all become a globe
the full of my spread legs
and between them
the centre is thickening
the lips are pursing out
I am speeding up

my hands are driving
my cunt is driving
I am zooming to my inner space
only one direction
I am in there
it is blowing out
ballooning out
quickly quickly
my self steering
my self steered
all a flow
all a rush
a tidal wave
wet on my fingers
heat running in my thighs
in my tail
my tail is spinning shaking swishing
I am the world
I am spinning
taking space
making whirlwinds out of space
I am space
I am spilling in
I am spilling out
I am coming
streaming steaming
coming out

P . M . T.

the weaTHeR iS swePT doWN
iT iS a puRPLe floWeR
peTaLS goiNG puTpuT
aT mY cheeKS aND haiR
iT iS wouND iN a rouGH sheeT

peoPLe beaR iN
buLGiNG buLLS eYeS
taLK tuRNS faCToRY wheeLS
         faCToRY wheeLS
claRRioN caRRioN caLL
iNSiDe mY nuT a kiNDLiNG thRoB

i haVe doNe wroNG aGaiN
leT sliP the waY i aM
leT free the rouGH woRD
aND theY staReD
no theY wouLD noT saY
    theY aRe kiND
    noT i

i waNT to shooT
spLiT the breaSTBoNe
i waNT to breaK the iNNoCeNT
proBe the cuNT oF
a siXTY-yeaR-oLD viRGiN
taKe a prieST'S priCK
beTWeeN mY liPS

giVe me a staTue
aND i'LL shaTTeR
aND theN mYSeLF

aND theN ruN heaDLeSS
oVeR a briDGe-eND

i aM woRTH a peBBLe
i aM woRTHY oF no looKS
                no proFeRReD haND
keeP youR faKe giFTS
i knoW wheRe youR haTe lieS
you waNT mY cuNT oN a diSH
YouR teeTH aRe baRe
beHiND youR smiLe

you wouLD woLF me
iF you couLD caTCH aND cooK me
buT i wieLD cleaVeR fiRST
aND buRST mYSeLF

hoW maNY skiNS haS a
suPeR suPeR-eGo

giVe uS a kniFe
giVe uS a scaLPeL
giVe uS a boDY
oN a scReaMiNG beD

yeS i wiLL toRTuRe
oNe mY eYeS
two buRN skiN iN ciGaReTTe steaKS
tiLL i aM raW raW reD
cuT oFF mY fooT
thRee riGHT
fouR leFT

duMP boDY
iN faST ruNNiNG waTeR

CRAWLING

I never knew so much could breed
from so little fornication.
My knickers are crawling
with green things and orange things
the murmur and thrust of a nation.

Long heads
long legs
see-through bodies
eating at me.
There they are laughing
leg on knee, saying
'Hee hee –
We spawned without sound
in the forest of G
we grew with the force of secrecy.
You won't kill us now
with soap and a towel.
We'll make you squirm
for your ecstasy.'

I slept with two
within two weeks
one silly, one insane.
I think it was the silly one
who drove me up a lane
and told me how he'd love to
with me then and then again.
And then he did and did again.
I know he didn't mean

to sow the seed of foreigners
among my home-grown fields.

Now, even though I smile and smile
those villains bite at me.
I can't reach down to scratch at them
while you're still there to see.
I've got some oil to burn them out
before they burn me down –
then it's back to sweet and wild romance –
It's just love's bitter crown!

ENGAGEMENT

If it weren't for
that honey-haloed
white-lighted
beam-through-fresh-open-blinds
look of yours
I would not have made your fable
your Aeneas and Naoise
glued in my own blue package.

If it weren't for
their hens' cluck –
'Oh he's lovely,
a sound man,
keeps you quiet' –
their shoving of rings
their man-only praise
I would never have worn you.

If it were only
your laughs
your deep down
oh-so-traditional honour
your sporting maleness
your permanent and prisoning job
I could have strolled full-directed
to the other side of the world.

NIGHTS WITH ANNE

nights with anne
and the headlights are on
and the alcohol flow
is rushing my head upriver
i'll escape this present
i'll fly to the moon and back

she has the pale brightest
pair of eyes so prophetic
that ever spoke spear
to my own dark horse

steal a saddle to another world
we are high-ho-thunder away
we are saved from
                    the wolfing plastics
                    the tin buttresses
                    the right attitudes
                    the feminine assent

strike a song there
for i and i am
in sudden ignition
my own bright key
my own fused force
propelled by me
not men not god
but the female whirl
is fuel to our moves
as we sing
raise cries

raise glasses
raise skirts
to the knee
to the waist
to the neck
to the head
to the
come on up baby
I'm home

THE GREENHOUSE EFFECT

I care about the Greenhouse effect. I really do. But it'd be great to combine ecology with a bit of excitement. I always go for the powerful ones, so I'm concentrating on the speaker. He's really composed and confident, talks like we were all sitting in his house. I like his pale blue eyes. Oh, I could sing him that song, 'Pale Blue Eyes'. There's no other girl in the room he'd think about, I reckon. The two attractive ones are with men. I could have him all right. Oh, but he's probably married. No ring, but that doesn't mean anything. Maybe he's doing it the ecological way, shacking up with a torrid, hippy beauty who makes clay ornaments, knits and sews all their clothes, makes gigantic tapestries and has their kitchen full of herbs and spices. He wouldn't have much time for my baked beans and sausages.

He has a slight beer belly. How, I wonder? Surely ecologists don't drink, not to excess anyway? It's a beautiful world all right, when I look at it. Of course O'Connell Street is a far cry from the Amazon. It's hard to picture all those trees, miles upon hundreds of miles of them. God, I'd love to see Brazil. What was that he said, 'wife'? No, no, he said something about life. I wouldn't mind living in West Cork among the natives; no need for electricity or anything. I'd feel like a god. He does. He doesn't look like he was born in the countryside. The faraway hills that used to be green, I suppose. Let's hie to the hee-lands!

He certainly seems to know his stuff. He's quoting figures now. 0.6% rise in temperature per annum, 1 foot rise in sea level.

'My god my melons,' says one woman.

If the city centre gets flooded, that's me upskuttled, not to mention all the poor people in the flats. Come to think of it, no-one *has* mentioned them.

'Of course,' says the curly-headed one, 'if people had to move from the city centre, that would affect us in the mountains.'

A sore place to be affected.

Now to the important bit. What to do about all this? Good question there from a Northern woman. They always get to the point.

'Lobby,' he says, 'lobby your politicians. If everybody in this room called to their local politician tomorrow, you'd be surprised at the difference it would make.'

I certainly would. Most of the people here haven't a clue what's going on or what to ask a politician to do – no more than myself.

'Don't spend money,' he says. 'The government should bear all the expense of atmosphere-friendly products. The government owes us. That's what we elected them for.'

What government is he talking about? He's English. My god, he actually wants someone else to take the reins, not to mention the responsibility. Some Sir Lancelot he is. I thought he rode to Dublin on a white pony. Turns out he drives a car on leaded petrol, has incandescent bulbs on his ceiling and cuts down trees for firewood. Ecology my foot. Some wild thing he is. There's no excitement here. I'm going home.

Looking at him again, I wouldn't say he'd be great in bed. His hips are the wrong shape. So is his head. Next time I want excitement I'll go to a disco.

F-ING OFF

Finally
I've finished
with your fucks
	your farts
	your filthy sheets
	your faked feelings
	your fluke grins
	your fluthered nights.

I've had it with
our frenzied foutering
in cars and fields
our fined-down fornication.

I'm frying our bond
on a full fire
and then flying free
to a new frontier.

KEEPING THE ANIMAL DOWN

that's the special welcome
eyes brilliant
hands buttered out
a house block-full of fires
heating to the roots of the hair

the wine is opened
dark red and viscous
splutters to the glass's brim
the roast smokes up the nostrils
browns succulently the tongue
that's home

then the blanketed hot-bottled bed
you sink sombre into
until you wish to wake

that's the shock
the first sound is a snort
or a bluster in the throat
next a chair is thrown to the wall
then a knock

familiar now
you remember old tricks
sit silent
lids lowered
while sparking eyes search you

take the apple spiked to your hand
and smile with
all your skin's face

no sudden move when you rise
just a smooth ascent
a quiet push back
from the board

that's the old burning
turning in a vessel kept still
that's keeping the animal down

ORIGINAL SIN

They tell me my child is a sinner
before he leaves the womb.
Well he must be a wizard
of a Hallowe'en tricker
if he sins while upside down
in a bag of water.

They say we made a sinner
because we made a sin
with the evil diction
of the mutual friction
of the basest parts
of our base bodies.

Now the woman's body is sin
and the baby lying within
is staring down
at the evil crown
of the pagan goddess, Quim?

No, says the Catholic priest,
you're having a pagan feast.
The child is a sinner
because of his flesh.
All human beings
are made of trash.
Every heart that beats
and is not baptised
is in Satan's drum,
synchronised.

So what about God
or is he too big
to jump in the womb
and be infra dig?

DNA is the greatest sin –
Duped with Natural Acumen –
There's my child
with a natural mind
and the churches want to put him
in a moral bind.

But it makes no odds
because my child's a bud
and she'll burst onto earth
like a flower should.
She'll shut up the church
like a jack-in-the-box
and she'll shout 'Up yours'
to the Pope and John Knox.

The Original Witch
will pick up the switch
and turn off the lights
in the steeple's sight.
She will laugh Ha Ha
She will laugh Ho Ho
And the walls will go
just like in Jericho.

BABY SKIN

My baby
you cling, I hope,
with resolution
through all these quakes
of mine.

I am riding a demon
when I remember.
My hand slips
to touch the swelling waist
that is you
and
suddenly
I see you,
pale and rounded,
sleeping like you know the world.

I reach your skin
and
teddy close
you hug me
blind
safe
into tears.

I would live forever to see your face.

FEEDING THE BABY

– there's a cat on the white line
– my racing car speeds up
– i brake
– the screech fills my head
– fills my head

I open my eyes.
The screech continues.
I had forgotten you in the corner,
your nightly serenade.
Only an hour's break this time
and you grate into my sleep,
turning the key in my back.
I am your pet robot.

I struggle to your cot,
lift your heated ball of a body,
heavier each feed,
Why did I have you?
Your fingers are soft as sausages,
I could bend them backwards.
Or your neck could crack
with an even flick.
You have made rivers of my breasts
where you float your smile.
Your chin flops like a drunken thing,
careless in greed.

Now the fiendish cholic cries
like ten unstopped alarms.
The trek begins.

I nearly dropped you then
when the heater flex grabbed my legs.
I almost threw you over my shoulder too.
My back was never so strained.
You are breaking me down.
If you don't stop,
I'll kill you
and then myself.

You calm to a whimper,
a heavy breathe on my back.
I check at the mirror.
Your eyes, dark and staring,
take in your world.
I look younger than I thought,
our faces an open locket.
Am I mother or child?
Your strange familiarity makes me tremble.
Perhaps you will be a great actor
when you grow.

SONG FOR AONGHUS

Who are you that have come in –
a stranger from another race
that have no face but you?
But are they still around you?
You are smiling at the ceiling,
at a room's empty space.

Who are you that have come in –
bringing inspiration home
as your body breathes
your spirit streams out?
I thought I had lost a life.
I thought the world was a straight line.

Who are you that have come in –
to start me swelling out again
when I had thought me flat?
You are pouring back in
through the lightning chink you made.
Your eyes are not mine
your hair is not mine
your sallying smile is all your own
and still they tell me
as I am spelled in awe
that you came from me
that I had you
that you are mine.

GERRY

I have come to claim my happiness
at your side.
You drew me in somehow
to kiss, I think, what life is
and look I am spreading out.
You did it in the dark
and what can I say?
You are straight out special
catkin beautiful
lush like green.

There is a dark spot by your side
where we are both alone watching.
Do you ever hate me those times,
you in need
I in battle gear,
when it comes to crunches
and I cannot say 'You –
I love you.'

You know the truth.
It's all a cloth I place on me
for fear I'll dust away.
I love the way you touch my hair
the way your words can flame
the gentle way you make a home
the power that builds from pain.
I think the world of women see
the bright blue loving self
that wants to tell me
where's my star

and when my ship is high.
And can I ever lead you in,
to fill your own worth out
to take and eat your own dear soul
and smile your own full mouth?

NOTHING FOR GIRLS

(*for Angela*)

First there is the childsong,
bright blue childsong,
ringing up the air.
You are the sky
and the bird and the cloud
and the scruffy earth
and the mole and the worm
and the world is all people.

Then there is the difference.
Rainbow childsong.
Colours have a place.
You still put faces
on the trees and mushrooms
but you begin to see borders,
where the sky, where play ends,
school begins.

Borders build a world.
Here's a country for under-twelves.
Here's the teenage nation.
There's the adult set,
they're called 'people'.
Children are sort of apprentice people,
so they don't understand,
so they have all these notions
about things being people
and colours having faces
and sums being boring
and they hate borders.

. . . and people kind of envy um
although they say they love um
and there's another thing
although they say they love um
they're always trying to change um
more like children love people
because they become like um . . .

Children never understand
why people feel so bitter.
I mean, that's what children aim for –
to be people.
But people are always sorry
they can't be children again.
Because when you're people
you must believe in borders
and don't believe your eyes
or your ears or anything you feel.

There's a little girl
who runs and shouts
and turns cartwheels
and wants to be an artist
and takes on all the boys
and beats them and loves it.
Doesn't see tomboy.
Doesn't see girl-not-boy
Doesn't see boy-not-girl
Sees people –
                    in a cartwheel
                    in a colour
                    in a sweat
                    in a treat

people hugging
people crying
people almost split from laughing
people people people . . .

There she is
in the comic shop
looking for herself
and sees nothing but borders,
what she is not,
what they are,
and suddenly she changes.
'Nothing,' she says, head down,
'Nothing for girls.'

EASTER 1989

I'm not the woman my great-grandmother was,
to stand on the stairs between her son
and the Tans.
'You'll kill me first,' she said.

I'm not the woman Bernadette was,
to slap an Englishman's indifferent cheek,
to come back from wounds that would
make a corpse.

I'm not the woman Máiréad was,
to burn out body and mind
in her people's cause,
to die without a home.

Always, on the border,
I wish I held the gun,
but time or place has made me small.
I think if they soldiered my streets,
searched me,
took my husband out,
I would fight.
But I have seen my father take my mother,
the law take my neighbour,
the church take my womanhood,
and I remain unbloodied.

Where I live, the battle is over.
We work to forget our crazed grandparents
and their mind for a nation
and their nights in ditches

and their songs of defiance.
Every day we retrench,
keep down our heads,
make deeper and wider the dividing line
between us and their hopes,
between us and their guns.
The proud republic they cried
and died for
is a whinging turncoat
picking their pockets
by the side of a new main road,
heading south.

And I am a woman
with children inside me,
bearing out my distance,
taking on my silence,
who will ask where I was
when justice was turned over
and our people murdered,
and whether I sat drinking
in a plush pub
talking money
while West Belfast bled.

THE FUCKING PONTIFF

The great environmental hurt
disturbs his Unholiness, the Godfather,
who stands and counts the trees
that are butchered
and begs in the name of himself
that we build not break.

Under his feet, he crushes
the fine-flowing serpent called woman
who knows how to make things grow.

His Most Senile Reverence defends
the world's two-thirds blessed poor
who are far from him
but always with us.
Educate their ignorance.
Eradicate their power.

Under his rule, he teaches
to exterminate women in millions
with his brain-bent lessons.

His Grovelling Eminence
kisses the arses of leaders
but not women. Let them
have children till their arses break
and he'll beatify their broken bones.

Under his body, a fiery witch
is stabbed through with his penile sceptre
behind the arras of the tabernacle.

His Fucking Unnatural Majesty
wanks to the high chant
of his sterile harem.
His sacred spunk butters the bread
they suck and savour.
Oh the ecstasy.

Under his throne, the witches are ready
to topple and turn him
            and fuck him
                fuck him
                fuck him

OUR STREETS

These are our streets.
If you are a woman don't look up.
If you do you'll meet the eyes
of idle macho boys.
That's provocation.
If you are a woman and you hear 'Hello'
keep your mouth shut,
your head unturned and cowed.
Huddle up.
Walk faster.
Walk faster.

These are our streets.
If you are a woman and it's night
wear a long coat and keep a
spray-can to hand,
your only hope.
If you are a woman and you hear a footstep
steadily behind, stay calm,
steal a look,
don't run.
Walk faster.
Walk faster.

At seventy years your sleep is slow.
Kitty feared the night since Martin died,
most the lonely feel of the single bed
she made downstairs.
One time, the lamp still on,
her Mills and Boon lost in her lap,
glasses just above her

hanging mouth,
she slept from two to four.
A sudden, fuller darkness woke her,
broke a dream of heaven.
There he was.
Who was?
smell of sweat
tangled hair
eyes of glass
matted coat
murky hands
smell of sweat
staring down
snatched the book
mocking grin
'sexy cunt'
threw her glasses
ripped her nightdress
took a knife
and led it down
her sagging body
'rub me mamma
rub me bitch'
smell of sweat
smell of shit
'please don't make me'
like a nightmare
no voice coming
down upon her
smell of shit
tore her open
split her flesh
gashed her bloody

60

there's no screaming
there's no finish
pierce on push
pierce on darkness
fading out with
pain of piercing
smell of shit
smell of blood

These are our streets.
If you are a woman you see your body
cut up stark at every hand and eye.
Breast here.
Leg there.
If you are a woman you are squared off
in paperback, pasted on the daily news,
on a leash.
Walk faster.
Walk faster.

These are our streets.
If you are a woman you can't drink alone
in pubs where men look
through dark pint glasses,
you're a whore.
If you are a woman and you walk the streets
for money as the ads advise,
you are guiding men astray.
Walk faster.
Walk faster.

In the air-conditioned office,
Sally is a glamour-bird.

Her boss is pleased that she wears Gucci,
starts at eight,
is never late for business dates
and always looks like
Cosmopolitan built her up.
Now and then they take the road to Wicklow
and in a lacy room
they make a certain sort of love
while his wife shops in London
and her town flat gathers a little dust.
A major merger looming,
off one day to Pittsburgh.
Sally looked a sweet treat,
all the big men said.
'Right,' said Roger,
'Take my key. She's a tiger.
She'll be expecting me.'

One o'clock.
The door let streak a light
across the floor.
'I'm all in satin and champagne,
you old ram.'
Up the light.
Three investors
bellies forward
suits of cotton
ties of silk
held her down
smell of smoke
'you can't hurt me
I'll tell Roger'
'cut your whinging

you're a kitten'
bent her over
smell of smoke
'give her what
she's always wanted'
stripped and saddled
bit and battered
not too badly
left her standing
up and down
in and out
smell of smoke
smell of shit
tore her open
split her flesh
gashed her bloody
there's no screaming
there's no finish
pierce on push
pierce on darkness
fading out with
pain of piercing
smell of shit
smell of blood

These are our streets.
If you are a woman you must drive
a pram on broken footpaths,
dragging little ones behind,
be always patient.
If you are a woman you must rear
and feed and care and wear well
to be admired.

In tight shoes,
how can you
Walk faster?
Walk faster.

These are our streets.
If you are a woman you must break the mould,
smash the flashy screen
that makes us meat for pricks
and not for joy.
If you are a woman you must fight
to choose to work, to dress, to fuck,
to look straight in the eye,
to stroll and not
Walk faster.

THIRTEEN YEARS DEAD

Thirteen years dead
and she still comes to me.
She says the old things –
'I hate this place
but I can't get out.'
But 'Mother, come away,'
I say.
I leave her waiting in the yard
or stirring at the range,
her large dark eyes
and her curling hair
and I wake to remember
what I have not done.

I have wished for her looks,
her bouncing wit,
her boundless, selfless love,
while I stood
in the no-woman's-land
between two persons,
fighting the least lovely war
with myself.
The family remember her excellence.
'Of course, she was a saint.'
And, wicked, I think how she laughed
and could have saved us.

Thirteen years dead
to patriarchy
and they return to him,
forget the huge battles
she fought to keep the smile

that made us happy.
But I am breaking through the
silent walls.
She came to me last,
a witch like me,
wrapped in power.
She spoke.

'You must travel
the unchartered path.
Your way is sin.
So is the way of death.
There is no church here
to build a proxy world
and make us hate the real.
I have not lived
so much as now.
Now I have my force.
It spirals in and about me
but breathes too late.
You must take my force
and live as I could not.'

She spun to a black tornado cone,
came over me and spinning
entered all my skin.
She is here now,
in the world of my self,
moving with me towards a life.
I can begin
to forget the smiling frustrations,
the perverse hopes for salvation.
There is no holding
now I have cut loose
and she has come away.

NEW POETRY TITLES
FROM
BLACKSTAFF PRESS

DADDY, DADDY
PAUL DURCAN

Critically acclaimed for his vibrant and eclectic 'poetry of the present moment', Paul Durcan is one of the most dramatically intense of modern Irish poets. Drawing its strength from its urgent treatment of a wide range of contemporary subject matter, his poetry is also striking for the subtlety and strangeness of its unique imagery.

Now in *Daddy, Daddy*, Durcan pushes out in a radical new direction, sounding new depths. Fusing the personal with the political, his angry response to violence and oppression in poems such as 'The Murder of Harry Keyes' and 'Shanghai, June 1989' is incisive and humane. Here also are love poems of all manner and kind; bizarre meditations on the nature of loneliness; poems of celebration of writers and artists like Primo Levi, Sylvia Plath and Paul Cézanne. And finally, in this collection's last group of poems, he embarks on an exploration of his relationship with his father, creating poetry that is compelling in its probing artistry and painful honesty.

'If Yeats were alive he'd hold Paul Durcan in great esteem ...
Durcan is a great poet in a mould rarely seen these days.'
Martin Booth, *Tribune*

'Durcan has developed a technique which embraces the colours and darknesses, the fashions and recurring concerns of personal, religious, social and political life in the 20th century, from parochial Ireland to the global village.'
Philip Casey, *Sunday Press*

198 x 129mm; 208pp; 0-85640-446-2; pb

£5.95

AFTER SEYMOUR'S FUNERAL
ROY MCFADDEN

Always notable for a certain elegant precision, Roy
McFadden's poetry has drawn much of its strength from his
obdurate refusal to revere the sacred cows of political and
literary life.

In these latest poems, he rejects the mere 'editing of
yesterdays' for a painstaking audit, accurately balancing the
exaltations and discomfitures of youth against the wry
self-knowledge of maturity. The result is writing of the high-
est order: elegiac, controlled and profoundly personal.

'McFadden remains at all times open-eyed, if seldom wide-eyed ... a
watchful presence, perceptive and unblinkered.'
Aidan Carl Mathews, *Irish Press*

198 x 129mm; 80pp; 0-85640-434-9; pb

£5.95

TRIO 6

ANGELA GREENE
OLIVER MARSHALL
PATRICK RAMSEY

Continuing Blackstaff's ground-breaking *Trio* series, this new poetry anthology presents the innovative work of three emerging Irish talents.

Angela Greene's powerfully visualised poems range from intricate studies of family life to work of intense lyricism. And through the vitality of their lucid domestic imagery, these poems confront death and loss. Breaking down the artificial division between the mundane and the visionary, the rich expression of her poetry is full of unexpected delights.

Oliver Marshall's carefully crafted work is by turns poignant and amusing. Exhibiting a sharp relish of words, the novel language of these poems is drawn from an eclectic range of sources – classical music, Christianity, European languages, Irish place names – and employed with unerring exactness. Whether surveying his immediate domain or tackling larger questions of faith and doubt, Marshall displays a sensibility that is both Irish and European.

Patrick Ramsey exercises a watchful and meticulous control of his subject matter. Firmly rooted in the landscape of Belfast, his poems evoke a powerful sense of place – 'Like anywhere, *here* is a place to build'. And in his diffident, gentle love poems, Ramsey's attention to the fine details of 'the ordinary' touches upon the emotions lying within silence.

198 x 129mm; 80pp; 0-85640-431-4; pb

£5.95

ORDERING BLACKSTAFF BOOKS

All Blackstaff Press books are available through
bookshops. In the case of difficulty, however, orders
can be made directly to the publisher. Indicate clearly
the title and number of copies required and send
order with your name and address to:

CASH SALES

Blackstaff Press Limited
3 Galway Park
Dundonald
Belfast BT16 0AN
Northern Ireland

Please enclose a remittance to the value of the cover
price plus: £1.00 for the first book plus 60p per copy
for each additional book ordered to cover postage and
packing. Payment should be made in sterling by UK
personal cheque, postal order, sterling draft or inter-
national money order, made payable to
Blackstaff Press Limited.

Applicable only in the UK and Republic of Ireland
Full catalogue available on request